C

C000064080

by Murray Ogilvie

L'ang**Syne**

PUBLISHING

WRITING *to* REMEMBER

Lang**Syne**

PUBLISHING

WRITING *to* REMEMBER

79 Main Street, Newtongrange,
Midlothian EH22 4NA
Tel: 0131 344 0414   Fax: 0845 075 6085
E-mail: info@lang-syne.co.uk
www.langsyneshop.co.uk

Design by Dorothy Meikle
Printed by Ricoh Print Scotland
© Lang Syne Publishers Ltd 2013

All rights reserved. No part of this publication may be reproduced, stored
or introduced into a retrieval system, or transmitted in any form or by any
means (electronic, mechanical, photocopying, recording or otherwise) without
the prior written permission of Lang Syne Publishers Ltd.

ISBN 978-1-85217-315-9

Cooper

SEPTS NAMES:

Copper
Coupar
Coupare
Couper
Couppa
Cowlpar
Cowlper
Cowpar
Cowper
Culpar
Cupar
Cuper
Cupir

Cooper

MOTTO:
Inclinata Resurgo
(Though abased, I rise again).

CREST:
An oak tree with a branch
borne down by a weight.

Chapter one:

The origins of the clan system

by Rennie McOwan

The original Scottish clans of the Highlands and the great families of the Lowlands and Borders were gatherings of families, relatives, allies and neighbours for mutual protection against rivals or invaders.

Scotland experienced invasion from the Vikings, the Romans and English armies from the south. The Norman invasion of what is now England also had an influence on land-holding in Scotland. Some of these invaders stayed on and in time became 'Scottish'.

The word clan derives from the Gaelic language term 'clann', meaning children, and it was first used many centuries ago as communities were formed around tribal lands in glens and mountain fastnesses.

The format of clans changed over the centuries, but at its best the chief and his family held the land on behalf of all, like trustees, and the ordinary clansmen and women believed they had a blood relationship with the founder of their clan.

There were two way duties and obligations. An inadequate chief could be deposed and replaced by someone of greater ability.

Clan people had an immense pride in race. Their relationship with the chief was like adult children to a father and they had a real dignity.

The concept of clanship is very old and a more feudal notion of authority gradually crept in.

Pictland, for instance, was divided into seven principalities ruled by feudal leaders who were the strongest and most charismatic leaders of their particular groups.

By the sixth century the 'British' kingdoms of Strathclyde, Lothian and Celtic Dalriada (Argyll) had emerged and Scotland, as one nation, began to take shape in the time of King Kenneth MacAlpin.

Some chiefs claimed descent from

ancient kings which may not have been accurate in every case.

By the twelfth and thirteenth centuries the clans and families were more strongly brought under the central control of Scottish monarchs.

Lands were awarded and administered more and more under royal favour, yet the power of the area clan chiefs was still very great.

The long wars to ensure Scotland's independence against the expansionist ideas of English monarchs extended the influence of some clans and reduced the lands of others.

Those who supported Scotland's greatest king, Robert the Bruce, were awarded the territories of the families who had opposed his claim to the Scottish throne.

In the Scottish Borders country – the notorious Debatable Lands – the great families built up a ferocious reputation for providing warlike men accustomed to raiding into England and occasionally fighting one another.

Chiefs had the power to dispense justice and to confiscate lands and clan warfare produced a society where martial virtues – courage, hardiness, tenacity – were greatly admired.

Gradually the relationship between the clans and the Crown became strained as Scottish monarchs became more orientated to life in the Lowlands and, on occasion, towards England.

The Highland clans spoke a different language, Gaelic, whereas the language of Lowland Scotland and the court was Scots and in more modern times, English.

Highlanders dressed differently, had different customs, and their wild mountain land sometimes seemed almost foreign to people living in the Lowlands.

It must be emphasised that Gaelic culture was very rich and story-telling, poetry, piping, the clarsach (harp) and other music all flourished and were greatly respected.

Highland culture was different from other parts of Scotland but it was not inferior or less sophisticated.

Central Government, whether in London or Edinburgh, sometimes saw the Gaelic clans as

"The spirit of the clan means much to thousands of people"

a challenge to their authority and some sent expeditions into the Highlands and west to crush the power of the Lords of the Isles.

Nevertheless, when the eighteenth century Jacobite Risings came along the cause of the Stuarts was mainly supported by Highland clans.

The word Jacobite comes from the Latin for James – Jacobus. The Jacobites wanted to restore the exiled Stuarts to the throne of Britain.

The monarchies of Scotland and England became one in 1603 when King James VI of Scotland (1st of England) gained the English throne after Queen Elizabeth died.

The Union of Parliaments of Scotland and England, the Treaty of Union, took place in 1707.

Some Highland clans, of course, and Lowland families opposed the Jacobites and supported the incoming Hanoverians.

After the Jacobite cause finally went down at Culloden in 1746 a kind of ethnic cleansing took place. The power of the chiefs was curtailed. Tartan and the pipes were banned in law.

Many emigrated, some because they

wanted to, some because they were evicted by force. In addition, many Highlanders left for the cities of the south to seek work.

Many of the clan lands became home to sheep and deer shooting estates.

But the warlike traditions of the clans and the great Lowland and Border families lived on, with their descendants fighting bravely for freedom in two world wars.

Remember the men from whence you came, says the Gaelic proverb, and to that could be added the role of many heroic women.

The spirit of the clan, of having roots, whether Highland or Lowland, means much to thousands of people.

Chapter two:

From Gogar to Nova Scotia

Little is known about the precise beginnings of the Cooper clan. However, those named Cooper, Couper, Cowper, Cowpar, Cupar or Coupar are all thought to be linked in one way or another.

Previously the names would have been spelt Cupir, Culpyre, Cypre, Coupare or Cypruin. Their original coat of arms suggested they arrived here from France, more specifically, Brittany. That coat bore fleur de lis and ermine. However the fleur de lis was later dropped, to be replaced by laurel. In more modern times the most common explanation for their origin suggests that the name was linked to the towns of Cupar in Fife or Coupar in Angus. Later the name came to be associated with the occupation of barrel maker.

The name is first mentioned in the 13th

century, with a number of recordings related to land ownership. The most significant is the signature of Symon Coupare of Berwickshire on King Edward's Ragman Rolls in 1296. This deed is conclusive proof that he and his family were of VIP status. The Ragman Rolls was the name given to a collection of agreements, laid out on four rolls of parchment, which King Edward the first of England imposed on Scottish nobility and landowners in return for deciding who should be the next king of Scotland.

However, it wasn't until the 17th century that the family started to become well known, when the Coupers became owners of the Gogar estate, which forms a part of modern-day Edinburgh. It is believed the Gogar landowners are descendants of Symon Coupare. Their association with the land began when Robert Logan of Restalrig was adjudged to have been involved in the Gowrie Conspiracy. This was an attempt to kidnap King James VI of Scotland in August 1600. Logan, who was the last Baron of Restalrig, sold his property at Nether Gogar to Adam

Couper, who took possession in 1601. Three years later Couper bought the rest of the estate and Gogar remained in his family's possession for the best part of 100 years.

Adam died in 1608 and the Gogar Estate passed to his oldest son, John. He married Helen Skene and set about creating a magnificent home for them to live in. There was already a substantial house on the estate which had been built in the fourteenth century. But John extended it in 1625, when it became known as Castle Gogar. It survives to this day as a Grade A Listed Building on the outskirts of Edinburgh. Its walled garden, stables, cottage, gate lodge and a bridge are still intact.

In the 1630s John Couper became a Baronet of Nova Scotia. This was a hereditary title which men of means could buy at that time. Nova Scotia was set up by Sir William Alexander of Stirling with permission from King James in 1621. His mission was to create a New Scotland on the east coast of North America, not unlike New England. The Baronets of Nova Scotia were

created as a settlement scheme. The land was
divided into provinces, which were sub-divided
into dioceses. Each diocese was divided into three
counties and each county into ten Baronies of
16,000 acres each. A Baronet paid 1000 merks for
his Barony and 2000 merks to maintain six soldiers in the colony for two years and received a
badge on an orange ribbon, which he could wear
round his neck. A merk was a Scottish silver coin
worth about two thirds of a Scottish pound, or
about one English shilling. But Sir John didn't
enjoy his new-found lofty status for too long.
In 1640 he died as a result of an explosion at
Dunglass Castle. Sir John had joined a force com-
manded by the Earl of Haddington fighting for the
Covenanters in the Second Bishops War.

Chapter three:

A Family at war

The Bishops Wars were fought between Scotland and England from 1639 to 1640 as a consequence of an attempt by King Charles I to reform the Church of Scotland. Opponents to these reforms became known as Covenanters. They had signed a covenant rejecting the notion that King Charles I was head of the church and stated that only Jesus Christ could hold that position.

King Charles, who had been born in Fife, inherited the throne in 1625. His father James VI of Scotland became James I of England in March 1603. At that time Scotland and England operated like two distinct countries ruled by the same monarch. They each had their own separate parliament, church, law courts and tax-raising powers. They could even go their own way on foreign policy. Outside the Highlands, where many retained their Catholic convictions, Scotland's religion was

Presbyterianism, a harsh strict form of Protestantism. King James believed that his rule had a higher authority than that of the church. Despite this he failed in his attempts to force the Scots to embrace his Episcopalian doctrine, which allowed the monarch to appoint bishops to the church.

The king was supported by, among others, the Bishop of Galloway. He just happened to be William Couper, a relative of Sir John's. He was born in Edinburgh in 1568. At the age of 12 he enrolled at the University of St Andrews and graduated with an MA three years later. After three years teaching at a school in Hertfordshire, he returned north and became a Church of Scotland minister based in Stirlingshire. Originally he was against the reformations proposed by King James and signed a protest to Parliament in 1606 against the introduction of Episcopacy. However, within two years he changed his mind and embraced the proposed changes. The king promoted him to the Bishopric of Galloway in 1612, which also gave him the title Dean of the Chapel Royal. This was a position held by the Bishop of Galloway since

1504 and provided him with authority over all the royal palaces in Scotland. William died seven years later and his descendants were later known as the Coupers of Fentounbarns, in the county of Haddington.

When King James died his son King Charles decided to finish the job. It took him 12 years but in 1637 he ordered that the Anglican Book of Common Prayer should be read in St Giles Cathedral, Edinburgh. The congregation was outraged. Many believed it was closer to Catholicism than Protestantism. There was a riot. Hostility to Charles continued to grow and seven months later, in February 1638, Scotland's National Covenant was published. This document, prepared with the full support of the nobility and land-owning class, proclaimed Scotland's opposition to the king's new prayer book. It was put on public view in Edinburgh and immediately attracted 60,000 signatures. Copies were taken throughout the country and many more signed up. The king pressed ahead regardless and this led to war. The First Bishops War began in January,

1639, and was effectively over six months later with the Covenanters victorious. On June 19, 1639 the two sides signed the Treaty of Berwick and Charles went back to London, apparently agreeing to let the Scots make decisions affecting religion. However, in January, 1640, Charles decided to have another attempt at subduing Scotland and the Second Bishops War took place. This time the Covenanters decided to go on the offensive and invaded England. Berwick was heavily fortified so the Covenanters bypassed it and headed for Newcastle. However, the Scots left a detachment behind under the command of the earl of Haddington to keep watch on the Border town in case its large army made a move. The Covenanters were victorious again, but tragically Sir John Couper died as a result of a mysterious accident at Dunglass Castle. The castle had been taken over by the Earl of Haddington and his forces to become their headquarters as they spied on the English garrison in Berwick. On August 30th, the Earl was standing in the courtyard reading a letter to his senior officers, which he'd just received from General Leslie, who was commander in chief of the Covenanters army. Suddenly there was a massive explosion in the gunpowder magazine. One of the castle walls collapsed onto the Earl and his officers, killing them all. An investigation into the incident suggested that it may have been no accident. There's a possibility that someone in the castle with English sympathies deliberately blew up the ammunition. The unnamed man perished in the explosion, but has the distinction of being one of the very first suicide bombers. The blast signalled the beginning of the decline for the Coupers of Gogar.

Sir John's son, also Sir John, inherited the estate. He was one of the Commissioners of the Scottish Parliament which approved the Treaty of Ripon. This was signed on October 14, 1640, and brought an end to hostilities. The agreement forced the English to pay the Scots £850 a day until a formal peace treaty was signed. In addition, the Scots would be reimbursed all their expenses incurred during the fighting.

In 1642 Charles decided to take on the

English Parliament in a battle for outright control south of the Border. This action began the first of three English Civil Wars between 1642 and 1651. The Scots Covenanters were convinced by Charles to get involved on his side. Their opponents were the Roundheads, led by a Huntingdon squire named Oliver Cromwell, who turned out to be a master tactician on the battlefield. The Royalists, led by Charles, lost and he was eventually beheaded. Cromwell did not spare his opponents, which was bad news for Sir John Couper. He had joined the battle against Cromwell and as retribution his rental income was taken away from him. His son, Sir John Couper the younger inherited the estate, but by now the family were in financial trouble. In 1685 he attempted to give away the lands of Gogar to his daughter Mary and her husband Thomas Chalmers. But this was blocked by his creditors and a lengthy legal battle ensued. Eventually in 1696 the Court of Session ruled against Sir John. Three years later the estate was sold by public auction to pay off the family debts. It was bought by a rich Edinburgh merchant, Andrew Myrton.

Around that same time Sir John died without a male heir and the title became dormant.

The title was revived in 1775 by his great grand-nephew, Sir Grey Cooper. He was a direct descendant of James Couper, the second son of the first Baronet. James became a minister and moved south to the Holy Island. Sir Grey was born in Newcastle Upon Tyne and went on to represent Rochester in Parliament and rose to become a Secretary to the Treasury.

He tried to buy back the Gogar Estate when it came up for sale in 1786. But the asking price of £42,000 was too high for him. Sir Grey was the fifth Baronet Gogar. When his grandson Sir Frederick, the seventh Baronet, died unmarried in 1850 the title became extinct.

That marked the end of the family's association with Gogar. However, by then they had re-established themselves in the west of Scotland. The third son of the first Baronet settled in Dunbartonshire. His descendants spread out over Ayrshire and West Stirlingshire. In the 18th century many changed their name to Cooper.

Chapter four:

Poet and Player

In 1828 the death of John Cowper was recorded. He was 91 and a farmer in the Abercrombie Estate in Fife, where his family had worked the land for over 300 unbroken years. It is to this family that one of England's greatest poets belongs.

William Cowper, who was born in November 1731 was one of the most popular English poets of his time. He made his name by writing about everyday life and countryside scenes. He suffered bouts of insanity as a young man and several times attempted suicide. He began his working life studying to be a solicitor but was unable to cope with the rigours. His first big break as a writer came when he was asked to contribute to a hymnbook. *Olney Hymns* was published in 1779 and includes "Praise for the Fountain Opened" and "Light Shining out of Darkness", which starts with "God moves in a mysterious way". He continued to write poetry and translated Homer's *Iliad* and *Odyssey* from Greek to English and some of his own verse into Latin. He died in 1800. Before his passing he wrote to a friend that his roots lay in Fife. "I am originally of the same shire, and a family of my name is still there," he confided.

Poetry was a word also used to describe the genius of another Cooper. In more recent times the most famous member of the extended clan was footballer Davie Cooper, who died tragically on on Wednesday March 22, 1995. He was born in Hamilton on Saturday February 25, 1956, and in primary school became captain of the football team. As he progressed to secondary school he was playing regularly in the local juvenile league. As a teenager he became a top amateur, while working as an apprentice printer. His first international honours came when he represented Scotland at the under-18 Home Nations Championship. Rangers, Motherwell, Clyde, Clydebank, Coventry City and Crystal Palace all wanted to sign him. But Davie had misgivings about going professional. However, he was eventually tempted to sign for lowly Clydebank in 1974, who were in the second division. His first four games for the club resulted in defeats, with him unable to make an impact. However in his second season he played in all of the Bankies 49 games, scoring 22 goals and helping the club get promoted to the first division. The following season he made his international debut for Scotland's under-21 side against Czechoslovakia. Cooper got three more caps that year, against Wales, Swizerland and England. By now he was in top form and he helped his club get promotion to the Premier Division, becoming the first Scottish club to win successive promotions. His brilliance alerted Rangers again and he signed for them in a £100,000 deal. It was suggested at the time that his signing on fee in 1977 was £10,000 and that his wages were £150 a week. It may not sound like much these days but back then it was a fortune. In his first season at Ibrox the club won the treble and he played in 52 of their 53 games. In the 1979 Drybrough Cup Final against Celtic he scored the goal which was voted the greatest ever Rangers goal by worldwide fans. He took the ball on his chest with his back to the goal, then proceeded to beat four defenders while playing keepie uppie, before slipping the ball into the back of the net. Ten years later his glittering Rangers career was over and he signed for Motherwell. He'd scored 75 goals in 540 games as a winger. Cooper spent four-and-a-half happy years at Fir Park before returning to his Clydebank roots as a player coach. He made his final appearance for the Bankies on February 21, 1995. A month later he was dead, after suffering a brain haemorrhage. At his funeral Walter Smith, who managed Rangers at the time, said, "God gave Davie Cooper a talent. He would not be disappointed with how it was used."

Chapter five:

Slaves in America

Official figures suggest as many as five million Americans claim Scots descent. However, it's estimated that figure could much higher, with the true number being possibly four times greater. Many of their forebears had arrived in the States during the 17th century. They'd gone to the new world seeking religious freedom and economic opportunities.

But thousands of Scots crossed the Atlantic not as settlers, but as slaves. They were sent there in shackles as a punishment for siding with the king against the forces of the victorious Oliver Cromwell in the English Civil War.

The first Scots slaves were captured after the Battle of Dunbar in September 1650. Cromwell's Parliamentary Army routed the locals who were loyal to King Charles II. Over 3000 Scots were killed and more than 10,000 were taken prisoner.

Half of them were set free because they were seriously wounded and posed no further military threat to the English, who went on to occupy Edinburgh. The rest were force-marched south to Durham. It took a week to get there and nearly half died along the way from their wounds or starvation. The survivors were jailed in Durham Cathedral and were not well cared for by their captors. During the weeks that followed cold, malnutrition and disease led to further loss of life. Over 5000 Scotsmen were taken from Dunbar but less than a third survived and they were transported to the new world as indentured servants. It meant they were forced to work in conditions akin to slavery for up to ten years before being released. Many of them found themselves in New England.

The next mass transportation of Scots slaves took place in the aftermath of the Battle of Worcester. About nine months after the Dunbar massacre Cromwell was still occupying Edinburgh and parts of lowland Scotland. Most of the Scots army still loyal to King Charles II were at Stirling, in an impregnable position. With the

Dunbar debacle still fresh in his mind, the Scottish commander, David Leslie, refused to launch another attack. King Charles, however, wanted to invade England, believing his loyal subjects would swell his forces. In July 1651 at Inverkeithing, on the north side of the Forth, the two armies clashed again. There were many casualties on both sides, but the English emerged victorious, again.

Cromwell was a master tactician and after Inverkeithing he appeared to have completely outwitted the Scots yet again. Instead of laying siege to Stirling his army headed north, apparently leaving England defenceless. When the Scots decided to take the bait and invade England he promptly about-turned and began chasing the royalists, who had deserted the safety of Stirling and crossed the Border at Carlisle.

Unfortunately, few Englishmen leapt to the king's cause, mainly because his Scottish soldiers were regarded as invaders rather than liberators. By the end of August the Scots were cornered at Worcester, where they fought a last-ditch battle against the Parliamentarians. The date

was September 3, 1651, exactly a year on from
the Battle of Dunbar. At the end of the conflict the
result was much the same, with 4000 royalist
fatalities and around 10,000, mostly Scots, in cap-
tivity. King Charles managed to escape to exile in
France, while David Leslie was sent to the Tower
of London for nine years. The prisoners were
marched to London and of those who survived
many were shipped to the new world as 10-year
slaves. Some joined their countrymen in New
England while others found themselves in
Virginia.

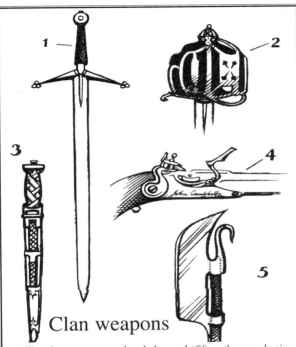

Clan weapons

1) The claymore or two-handed sword *(fifteenth or early sixteenth century)*
2) Basket hilt of broadsword made in Stirling, 1716
3) Highland dirk *(eighteenth century)*
4) Steel pistol *(detail)* made in Doune
5) Head of Lochaber Axe as carried in the '45 and earlier

GATHERING OF THE CLANS

CLAN MEMORABILIA FROM LANG SYNE

Books, postcards, Teddy bears, keyrings, mugs and much more...

Visit our website:
www.langsyneshop.co.uk

or write to us:
Lang Syne Publishing,
79 Main Street, Newtongrange,
Midlothian EH22 4NA
Tel: 0131 344 0414   Fax: 0845 075 6085
E-mail: info@lang-syne.co.uk